HOW TO MEET & DEFEAT THE ENEMY

The Keys To Victory In Spiritual Warfare

BLAKE CARROLL

Foreword by
James T. (Jimmy) Draper, Jr.

PublishAmerica
Baltimore

ISBN: 1-4241-0953-1
PUBLISHED BY PUBLISHAMERICA, LLLP
www.publishamerica.com
Baltimore

Printed in the United States of America

Acknowledgments

I want to express my deepest gratitude to the people whose encouragement, support, and diligent work helped make this book possible: Angela Bellacosa and Nancy Box, my gracious editors, James T. (Jimmy) Draper, Jr., my beloved mentor, and all of the wonderful staff at Publish America. You all are the greatest friends in the world.

Dedication

This work is dedicated first of all, to my Lord and Savior Jesus Christ; secondly, to my wonderful wife, April, and my two precious daughters, Taylor and Maddie; and finally, to my dad and mom, Lynn and Janice, my brother, Darren, my beloved grandparents, Deward and Martha Carroll, Dr. Troy, and Mary Lee Frye. I love you all so very much!

CONTENTS

Foreword

It has been my privilege to know Blake Carroll for several years now. I have spent time with him, been in his home and preached in his church. I have found him to be a young man of impeccable integrity, with a passionate love for the Word of God, a deep determination to see Christians grow in their faith, and a driving desire to see the lost come to faith in Christ. His preaching is solidly founded upon the Word of God. His warmth and genuine love for people comes across in his ministry.

This book that he has written deals with the battle that every Christian must engage in. We may not recognize it, but we are at war with Satan and his forces. Ephesians 6 gives us our battle plan and strategies. Blake Carroll has done a splendid job in opening this passage up for us to see the reality of the battle and the weapons of our engagement.

I commend these pages to you. Read them and you will be challenged and blessed. You will become equipped for the warfare that rages against us in our world today. And pass this on to others, as that is the specific command for us from God's Word: "What you have heard from me in the presence of many witnesses, commit to faithful men who will be able to teach others also" (2 Tim. 2:2).

Jimmy Draper
President, LifeWay Christian Resources

PART 1

BRACE YOURSELF FOR BATTLE

Finally, my brethren, be strong in the Lord and in the power of His might. Put on the whole armor of God, that you may be able to stand against the wiles of the devil. For we do not wrestle against flesh and blood, but against principalities, against powers, against the rulers of the darkness of this age, against spiritual hosts of wickedness in the heavenly places. Therefore take up the whole armor of God, that you may be able to withstand in the evil day, and having done all, to stand.

Stand therefore, having girded your waist with truth, having put on the breastplate of righteousness, and having shod your feet with the preparation of the gospel of peace; above all, taking the shield of faith with which you will be able to quench all the fiery darts of the wicked one. And take the helmet of salvation, and the sword of the Spirit, which is the word of God; praying always with all prayer and supplication in the Spirit, being watchful to this end with all perseverance and supplication for all the saints—and for me, that utterance may be given to me, that I may open my mouth boldly to make known the mystery of the gospel, for which I am an ambassador in chains; that in it I may speak boldly, as I ought to speak (Ephesians 6:10-20, NKJV).

Throughout one of the gloomiest periods of the Second World War, following the collapse of France and prior to America's involvement,

Winston Churchill wrote that the question in the minds of both friends and foes was this: "Will Britain surrender too?" At that time he made a speech that included this statement: "What General Weygand called the Battle of France is over. I expect that the Battle of Britain is about to begin. Upon this battle depends the survival of Christian civilization."[1]

It has been said, "The Christian life is not a playground—it's a battleground." Therefore if you are a Christian, you are in a battle on this battlefield. Upon this battle depends the serenity of your heart, the satisfaction of your marriage, the safety of your children, the security of your home, and the success of your life.

You are engaged in spiritual warfare. However, many Christians, perhaps more than care to admit, do not even realize it. In fact, this is a key problem. Many of God's soldiers are asleep in the barracks when they ought to be aggressively attacking on the battlefield. The cause for many Christians losing their battle with Satan on a daily basis is they are not even showing up for the war. As a matter of fact, it appears as though many Christians do not even realize there is a war waging.

I once heard about a driver who was obviously drunk and heading the wrong way down a one-way street when a policeman pulled him over. "Didn't you see the arrow, buddy?" the policeman asked. "An arrow?" the puzzled driver said. "I didn't even see the Indians."

I am gravely troubled because there are a lot of Christians who don't realize who their enemy is; they don't realize there is a war waging; they do not understand that every single day they are in a fight for their spiritual life. Someone has stated the problem well: "Much of the church's warfare today is fought by blindfolded soldiers who cannot see the forces ranged against them; who are buffeted by invisible opponents and respond by striking one another."

The great military general, Douglas MacArthur, said in his 1951 farewell address to Congress, "In war there is no substitute for victory." That statement is certainly applicable in the spiritual warfare we find ourselves in as born-again believers. If you are a Christian, I want you to know that in your war, it is God's sovereign will for you to be triumphant. Furthermore, it is about time that many Christians stop regretfully retreating and begin courageously charging. There are too many of God's children who are letting the devil defeat them when they ought to be defeating the devil.

Adrian Rogers, the pastor emeritus of Bellevue Baptist Church, once told the true story of a football player who graduated from college. The coach then asked him if he would like to come on staff, be a scout, and try to find other good football players. He said, "Sure coach, what kind of a player are you looking for?"

The coach replied, "Well, there's the kind of guy that when you knock him down, he just stays down."

He answered, "We don't want him, do we, coach?"

The coach said, "No, we don't want him. But then there's the kind of guy that when you knock him down, he gets up. But if you knock him down the second time, he just stays down."

The man answered, "We don't want him either, do we, coach?"

The coach said, "No, we don't want him either. But there's the kind of guy that when you knock him down, he gets up; you knock him down, and he gets up; you knock him down again, and he just keeps getting up."

The man answered, "Now that's the guy we want, right, coach?"

The coach said, "No, we don't want him either. What I want you to do is find the guy who's knocking all these other guys down. That's the guy I want."

I personally think it is high time that Christian people get off of the defense and go on the offense. Far too many Christians are staggering into heaven as crushed saints, when they ought to be soaring into heaven as conquering soldiers. In the following chapters, I want to share with you how to brace yourself for battle on a day-to-day basis so that you can be victorious in this spiritual conflict.

CHAPTER 1

REALIZE THE FIGHT
YOU WAGE IN LIFE

This war is very different from other wars that have been waged in history, simply because it is a spiritual war. In his epistle to the Ephesians, the Apostle Paul wrote, "For we do not wrestle against flesh and blood, but against principalities, against powers, against the rulers of the darkness of this age, against spiritual hosts of wickedness in the heavenly places" (Eph. 6:12, NKJV).

The fight that Paul is speaking of is going on at this very moment, right now in your life. Now understand that you may not be able to see the bullets that are continuously being fired, or the bombs bursting in the atmosphere above you, but the war is real just the same. It is being fought in your home. Today, that is why we see Christian marriages falling apart in record numbers, and also why Christian children are defying the authority of their parents.

This war is waging in your head. That is why even preachers of the Gospel are being thrown into the prison of pornography and being ambushed by adultery. It is taking place in your heart. That is why all of us have to genuinely struggle every single day to be virtuous rather than violent. However, just because this war is imperceptible does not suggest that it's nonexistent. If you don't believe there is a war raging, just take a look at your morning newspaper and you will see the effects of this war in such things as drug abuse, murder, prostitution, rape, terrorism, theft, and child molestation. These are the dreadful displays that are exhibited by this horrendous war.

You must also realize that every single Christian is in this war; every Christian has to go to battle. There are no deferments and no discharges in God's army. If you are a Christian, you better get ready to fight because you're "in the army now."

Paul clearly stated, "we do *not* wrestle against flesh and blood …" (Eph. 6:12, NKJV; emphasis added). So take into consideration that when you give your heart and life to Jesus Christ, you do not get into a club, you get into a conflict. Besides, God not only puts salvation in your heart, He puts a sword in your hand. When Paul came to the end of life's journey, he said, "I have fought the good fight" (2 Tim. 4:7, NKJV). He also exhorted young Timothy, his son in the ministry, "to fight the good fight of faith" (1 Tim. 6:12, NKJV).

I want to reiterate that the problem is, we have got too many so-called "soldiers of the Cross" who are asleep in the barracks rather than fighting on the battlefield, and many of whom give up without even firing the first shot. In fact, there are perhaps some of you reading this book wondering what I'm talking about, because you never feel like you're engaged in a war. Thus, the reason many of you don't feel that you're a part of this war is because you have put down your weapons and essentially gone the way of the world. To tell the truth, the reason you and the devil get along so well is that you are both roaming the same road.

I want you to know that if you are a blood-bought, born-again child of God, you are in the war. You may be a runaway, you may be a deserter, you may be AWOL, but you are in the war nonetheless. You cannot straddle the fence in this war. You cannot be like Switzerland; you cannot remain neutral. You're either on one side or the other. You are either for God or against God. There is absolutely no middle ground. Therefore, you had better be on your guard at every moment, and realize the fight you wage in life.

CHAPTER 2

RECOGNIZE THE FOE YOU
WRESTLE IN LIFE

General Douglas MacArthur, whom I mentioned earlier, once wrote a tremendous article entitled "Requisites for Military Success," in which he gave the four specific requirements that he considered imperative to fulfill in order to be victorious in battle.

First of all, he said that there must be morale: a will to win, an esprit de corps, a cause worth dying for. Secondly, there must be strength: capabilities, adequately trained and well-equipped personnel. Thirdly, he said there must be an adequate source of supply. Lifelines must be kept open so that those at the front can obtain all that they need to conquer and defeat the enemy. However, he said that the most important principle was this: "The greater the knowledge of the enemy, the greater the potential of victory."

The Apostle Paul tells us exactly who our enemy is. He says, "Put on the whole armor of God, that you may be able to stand against the wiles of THE DEVIL" (Eph. 6:11, NKJV). Now I must be very careful as I discuss the devil. Often it seems as though people tend to go to one of two extremes when thinking of the one called Satan. For example, on the one hand, many people pay no attention to the devil; some even make light of him. They visualize the devil as some type of mythological figure, like Santa Claus or the Tooth Fairy. In fact, I once heard about two six-year-olds that struggled with the problem of the existence of the devil. One boy said, "Oh, there isn't any devil." The other, rather upset, said, "What do you mean, there isn't any devil? It talks about him all the way through the Bible!" The first replied, "Oh, that's not true, you know. It's just like Santa Claus; the devil turns out to be your dad." But I want you to know unashamedly that Satan is not merely a flesh-and-blood human, nor is he a perception of evil. He is a living, personal, literal being with the ability to control people and to carry out many evil deeds. There is a personal devil, just as there is a personal God.

However, there is another extreme we should avoid when thinking of the devil, and that is the extreme of being overzealous about him. There are some Christians who are absolutely fanatical when it comes to the devil. One time I read about a woman that went to a church picnic, where the ladies were having a covered dish luncheon. When she walked in, one of these super spiritual ladies walked up to her and said, "What did you bring for lunch?" She said, "Deviled eggs." Well, without delay this woman flung her hands up and shouted, "I bind everyone of them in the name of Jesus!" But I like what this dear lady said back to her. She said, "You can bind them all you want to, but they're still deviled eggs." As someone once said, "I want to give the devil his due, but I don't want to give the devil the farm." You definitely need to know who he is. We are plainly told in Ephesians 6:12 that our battle is against "spiritual hosts of wickedness in the heavenly places." So that tells me that Satan is a spiritual being, but it also tells me that not everything spiritual is inevitably good. But it shouldn't shock you that your fight is spiritual, because your foe is spiritual as well.

Now you can't fight Satan on a natural plain; he must be fought on a supernatural plain. You need to realize that you cannot win your war against Satan by total determination alone. He shakes at the sight of the breastplate of righteousness. He shivers before the shield of faith. He shudders before the sword of the spirit. But those are the only weapons that he is afraid of, and those are the only weapons that will work because he is a spiritual foe.

The devil is not an enemy to be played with. The Word of God tells us that our war is against "principalities, against powers, against the rulers of the darkness of this age" (Eph. 6:12, NKJV). Therefore, don't underestimate the power of the devil. Don't ever assume that you can deal with him on your own, because you can't. By yourself, in your human flesh, he will always defeat you.

We are also admonished to "stand against the *wiles* of the devil" (Eph. 6:11, NKJV; emphasis added). The Greek word for "wiles" gives us our English word "method." It literally means "deceit or trickery." The New International Version translates it this way: "Take your stand against the devil's schemes." Satan has been called "the master of deception." In fact, he has even deceived us in the way we envision him. When we hear someone speak of the devil, we normally conjure up the picture in our mind of a little man wearing long red underwear, with horns on his head, a forked tail, and a pitchfork in his hand, walking around looking for somebody bending over. A lot of people will look at a picture of the devil on the side of a deviled meat food product and remark, "I don't believe in that kind of devil." Well, I want to be totally honest. I don't believe in that kind of devil either.

Second Corinthians 11:14 says that "Satan transforms himself into an angel of light." If you could see the devil right now in bodily form, it would surprise you how delightful he would look. It would even surprise you how kind and courteous he could seem to be. As a matter of fact, you would never know that he is the most evil force on the planet.

You need to know that this devil is only interested in evil and obscurity. We are so keen on saying that "God loves you and has a glorious plan for your life." Perhaps we should add to that this reminder: "Satan hates you and has an evil plan for your life." You can mark this down. You can take this to the bank, and it will definitely draw interest. The devil is doing everything he can at this very moment to either take you to hell or, if you're going to heaven, to make your journey miserable.

God wants you to be victorious and virtuous. Satan wants you to be sad and sinful. If you are not saved, he will do all that he can to make certain you go to hell; and if you are saved, he will do everything he can to make you sin and cause you to lose the joy of your salvation. As I converse about the devil, I understand that many of you could be intimidated because he is so compelling. But that is why we need not ignore the last principle in the following chapter.

CHAPTER 3

RECEIVE THE FREEDOM
YOU WANT IN LIFE

You should appreciate the benefits and blessings you have in Christ Jesus, and claim the victory that rightly belongs to you and every other Christian. Paul says, "Put on the whole armor of God" (Eph. 6:11, NKJV). Literally what he is saying is this: "Put on the whole armor of God and keep it on." In this spiritual conflict, there are no cease-fires. There are no furloughs. There are no leaves of absence. There are no truces. You have got to keep your armor on and your guard up. You can never rest. You can never relax. You can never let your guard down; because if you do, Satan will surely sucker-punch you where it hurts. He will attack you at your weakest moment when you are least expecting it.

Thus I am telling you Satan is fierce. The devil is fatal. Old Lucifer is ferocious. This wicked one is frightening. But carefully note that he is not invincible.

Many people were terrified of Saddam Hussein prior to the first Gulf War, and they thought he would be such a daunting foe. But after the war was over, in just a matter of hours, General Norman Schwarzkopf stood before a press conference and gave this evaluation of old Saddam: "Saddam is neither a strategist, nor is he schooled in the operational arts, nor is he a tactician, nor is he a general, nor is he a soldier; other than that he is a great military man."[2] Likewise, Satan is not omnipotent; Satan is not omnipresent; Satan is not omniscient; but God is all three. Satan is not sovereign, but God is. But other than those characteristics, he is a mighty foe. However, 1 John 4:4 declares, "He who is in you is greater than he who is in the world." We have an advantage over the devil; it is the armor of God, and if used correctly, can give us the freedom we all want in life.

Imagine that you were sitting on a warship and putting your hand against the wall, which is actually called the "bulkhead." If you hold your hands 24 inches apart, that illustrates how thick some of the walls are on older battleships. In fact, the armor plating on an American battleship is so thick that a Russian Styx missile would bounce off an armor-plated bulkhead on a direct hit.

Armor on a ship is always placed in areas where the ship is the most vulnerable to enemy missiles. Usually, an armor belt is placed around the sides of the ship from about ten feet below the water line to just above the water line. Hypothetically, a torpedo hitting the armor belt would not penetrate the hull and cause flooding. Likewise, armor plating would be placed along the upper surface of the ship to repel bombs dropped from enemy planes. Furthermore, God has given you a suit of armor guaranteed to repel the most powerful missiles, the strongest bombs, and the mightiest torpedoes that Satan can fire your way. Is it any wonder that James said, "Resist the devil and he will flee from you..." (Jas. 4:7, NKJV)? There is not one single verse in the Word of God that tells us that we are to run from the devil. It says we are to flee temptation; we are to flee sin. But God's Word never says we are to flee from the devil. It plainly states that we are to resist the devil and he will flee from us.

Geoffrey C. Ward, in his book, *The Civil War*, tells a story about a scene that took place on a battlefield during the battle of Gettysburg:

Right in the middle of the Battle of the Wilderness, all the staff men who had been fighting in the east all this time-Grant had just come from the West-kept talking "Robert E. Lee, Robert E. Lee. He'll do this, he'll do that, and he'll do the other." Ulysses S. Grant heard all he wanted to hear and finally said to them, "I am tired of hearing about Robert E. Lee. You would think he was going to do a double somersault and land in our rear. I want you to quit thinking about what he is going to do to you, and I want you to start thinking about what you're going to do to him."[3]

You are in a war. It is a spiritual war and you have to brace yourself for battle. So you need to begin by thinking about what you can do to the devil, rather than what he can do to you. Because of the Lord Jesus Christ and His sacrificial death on the cross of Calvary, because of the amazing power of the Holy Spirit, and because of the armor of Almighty God, you can be victorious in this war and possess the freedom you want in life.

PART 2

SPIRITUAL ARMOR
FOR A SPIRITUAL ASSAULT

Therefore take up the whole armor of God, that you may be able to withstand in the evil day, and having done all, to stand.

Stand therefore, having girded your waist with truth, having put on the breastplate of righteousness, and having shod your feet with the preparation of the gospel of peace; above all, taking the shield of faith with which you will be able to quench all the fiery darts of the wicked one. And take the helmet of salvation, and the sword of the Spirit, which is the word of God...(Ephesians 6:13-17, NKJV).

The Andy Griffith Show has always been one of my favorite television shows. One of my all-time favorite episodes was when Andy told his son, Opie, the electrifying story of the American Revolution. He shared with Opie how in the year 1775, a man by the name of Paul Revere made his perpetual mark in history by a single horse ride. He knew that his nation was on the brink of war, and he did not want them to be caught by surprise. He knew the enemy was coming; however, he didn't know whether it would be by land or by sea. But very late on a moonlit night, when he saw those lanterns burning in the tower of the old North Church in Boston, Massachusetts, he immediately knew that the enemy was coming by land. At that point, he jumped on his horse and began to fearlessly ride him from village to village, sounding an alarm that would not only wake up the nation, but would wake up the world as he cried out, "To arms! To arms! The British are coming."

Without delay, I am sounding another alarm to you so that you might awaken to the reality that there is a war going on and your enemy is advancing. I am calling you aggressively to arms, not because the British are coming, but because the devil is already here.

It is so fascinating that the devil is introduced in the book of Genesis as a serpent. In 1999, the *New England Journal of Medicine* published a study concerning people bitten by dead snakes. This study included comprehensive research from Drs. Jeffrey Suchard and Frank LoVecchio of the Good Samaritan Regional Medical Center in Phoenix, Arizona. Both of these toxicologists suggested, "Education to prevent snakebites should include warnings against handling recently killed snakes."

In this remarkable study, Suchard and LoVecchio recounted the case of one such patient, who "shot a rattlesnake, striking the head several times, and observed no movement (in the snake) for 3 minutes." However, upon lifting the apparently "lifeless" creature, the man felt the snake sink its fangs deep into his right index finger.

The Phoenix researchers found that "rattlesnake heads are dangerous 20 to 60 minutes after decapitation." Based on their own experience in treating snakebite victims, the authors warned that "imminently fatal injuries do not prevent rattlesnakes from producing serious or even multiple envenomations."[4]

Now we know Lord Jesus dealt Satan a fatal blow at the cross of Calvary; however, he is still harmful, and we must continually be on our guard against him.

Just as Satan is a supernatural adversary, he requires supernatural artillery. Paul denotes in 2 Corinthians 10:4 that "the weapons of our warfare are not carnal but mighty in God for pulling down strongholds." In other words, what Paul tells us is that Satan is not afraid of bullets or missiles. He is only afraid of those supernatural weapons that are found in the armor of God.

In Ephesians 6, Paul shares with us in detail what we are to arm ourselves with in this war that we fight everyday. There are six pieces of equipment that make up this armor: the first five are for our guard against Satan, but the sixth one is so that we might go on the attack and defeat Satan.

You need to understand that Satan is definitely on the attack, because Paul cautions us to beware of the "fiery darts of the wicked one" (Eph. 6:16, NKJV). Satan has a quiver full of fiery darts, flaming arrows that he fires at us everyday from every imaginable angle. Now the good news is none of these can reach us or hurt us as long as we are equipped with the full armor of God because each piece of this armor is purposely designed to defend against any specific dart that Satan throws our way.

CHAPTER 4

THE BELT OF TRUTH
REPELS THE DART OF DECEIT

The first piece of equipment that a Roman soldier would put on was what would be called a girdle or a belt. Paul wrote: "Stand therefore, having girded your waist with truth..." (Eph. 6:14, NKJV). The belt was not simply a strip of cloth around the waist, but rather was a leather apron that helped protect the lower part of the soldier's body. To this belt was fastened all of the other pieces of the armor. The soldier would then gather up the tunic, or long robe that he was wearing, and tuck it into this belt so he would not be stalled in the fight.

The belt of truth represents God's holy Word. In Ephesians 1:13 Paul refers to "the word of truth." As a matter of fact, Jesus said in John 17:17, "Your word is truth." In this case God's Word is a defensive weapon. It is to be used to repel the dart of deceit.

Jesus made a statement about the devil in the eighth chapter of John that is rather interesting. He said, "He is a liar and the father of it" (Jn. 8:44, NKJV). Satan is genuinely deceitful and is the master of deception. It was his deceit of Eve that fated the whole human race. In fact, Paul said in 1 Timothy 2:14, "And Adam was not deceived, but the woman being deceived, fell into transgression." Therefore, the same devil that could deceive Eve in the Garden of Eden can deceive you and me where we are right now.

Think about this. Satan has his doctrines just as God has His doctrines. We are expressly cautioned in 1 Timothy 4:1, "Now the Spirit expressly says that in latter times some will depart from the faith, giving heed to deceiving spirits and doctrines of demons." So take time to understand there is demonic doctrine just as there is divine doctrine. You are not affixed to God securely by the belt of His truth. If you are not extremely careful, you will be "tossed to and fro and carried about with every wind of doctrine."

We are essentially living in a day and age where you had better be able to identify false doctrine. I have known many Christians throughout my ministry who have fallen prey to demonic cults because they could not properly identify false doctrine.

A Sunday school teacher once asked one of her pupils, "What is false doctrine?" A spirited little boy raised his hand and said, "It's when the doctor gives the wrong stuff to people when they're sick and they die." Now that is rather humorous; however, there is great truth to that because false doctrine will kill you.

You had better put on the belt of truth every single day, because just as soon as you take it off, you will be caught with your pants down. And that is when Satan will poke a pitchfork in you right where it hurts. The word of God is truth. The Bible is not God's Word because it is true; it is true because it is the Word of God. In fact, God does not say something because it is true; something is true because God says it is. Therefore, no matter what you hear from any pulpit, any professor or any preacher, if it does not line up with the Bible, it is not truth.

The reason the devil hates the Bible so much is because it is the word of truth. One Bible scholar made this incisive remark: "Satan does not waste his ammunition. Professors who are being paid to teach philosophy, English, biology, or mathematics often take time from their class periods to undermine the Bible and orthodox Christianity. Why are they not doing the same thing with the sacred books of other religions? The answer is that Satan, the original liar, is sympathetic with books that lie. His real enmity is directed against the book of truth, because it contains the dynamite for his defeat." Daily we must surround ourselves with the belt of truth, which is the Word of Almighty God. When we do that, we can fearlessly enter this spiritual conflict, knowing the devil is powerless against us.

CHAPTER 5

THE BREASTPLATE OF RIGHTEOUSNESS REPELS THE DART OF DISGRUNTLEMENT

After we equip ourselves with the belt of truth, we must "put on the breastplate of righteousness" (Eph. 6:14b, NKJV). The breastplate was a coat of mail that covered the front and back of the soldier's body from the neck to the thighs. It was designed to protect the most vital organ of the body, the heart, from injury.

Your heart is the real "heart of the battle" in this war. Understand that in the Word of God, the heart represents the will, the emotions, and the mind. It is the core of what we are. As a matter off fact, your eternal destiny will be decided in your heart. Romans 10:9 says, "If you will confess with your mouth the Lord Jesus and believe in your *heart* that God raised Him from the dead, you shall be saved" (emphasis added).

How you think, how you act, the person you are, or the person you will soon become, is always decided in your heart. Psalms 23:7 states, "As a man thinks in his heart, so is he." So the heart of Satan's attack is the attack of the heart. Let me share with you how Satan works in this area of our warfare. Satan will come to your heart and try to tempt you to sin. The moment you do, he will point his bony finger of condemnation at you because you did. He is the "accuser of the brethren," and he loves to remind us of our sins. He loves to bring them up to our attention. He loves to dig up old dirt and throw it in our face. He loves to rattle the skeletons in our closet, and he does that until we become doubting Christians and then, finally, pouting Christians.

I cannot stress to you enough how vitally important it is that you put on the breastplate of righteousness. Because when you do, you can differentiate between Holy Spirit conviction and satanic accusation. Understand that the Holy Spirit will use the Scripture to convict us, but Satan will use feelings to condemn us. When the Spirit convicts us, it is to draw us closer to God and make us more like Christ; but when Satan condemns us, it is to steer us away from God and make us more like the world. Spiritual conviction leads to admission and adjustment, but satanic accusation leads to despair and disillusionment. Notice the Spirit will convict you of unconfessed sin in your life so that you can get right with God, but Satan will charge you with sins you have already confessed so that you will not feel right with God. When this happens, and it happens to the best of us, you must take up the breastplate of righteousness. Now let me tell you what that implies. When the Word of God speaks of righteousness, it refers sometimes to positional righteousness, and it refers sometimes to practical righteousness. Moreover, we must note the difference. When God saves you, He declares you righteous once and for all. We call that justification. However, there is also the righteousness that God wants to manifest in your life daily. We call that sanctification. So we need both of these kinds of righteousness in order to repel the devil's dart of disgruntlement.

The Bible declares in 2 Corinthians 5:21 that we are "the righteousness of God in Christ." Therefore the next time Satan comes to you with the dagger of disgruntlement in his hand and tries make you think you are not right with God, you make sure you are equipped with the breastplate of righteousness. You just simply say to him, "Satan, I am the righteousness of God in Christ Jesus, and nothing you can say or do to me will ever change that." Do you know what will happen? The dagger of disgruntlement will shatter in his hand against the breastplate of God's righteousness on your heart.

CHAPTER 6

THE GOSPEL OF PEACE
REPELS THE DART OF DISCORD

The Apostle Paul tells us in Ephesians 6:15 to "shod our feet with the preparation of the gospel of peace." One of the most significant pieces of equipment for a soldier was his boots. Without good boots he could not march, and without good boots he could not do battle. In Paul's day, the Roman soldier wore sandals that were firmly fastened to his feet by leather thongs. On the soles of these sandals were bits of metal, or hobnails, to give the soldier a firm footing on the ground. It was very important for a solider to keep his footing, because no soldier can wage war flat on his back.

That is why we are told that we must have our feet "shod with the preparation of the gospel of peace." This peace is the peace that comes from receiving the gospel and knowing that Jesus Christ is your Lord and Savior. Romans 5:1 says, "Therefore, having been justified by faith, we have peace with God through our Lord Jesus Christ." Now ponder that verse for a moment. In truth, if you are at peace with God, you are at war with the devil. You should now understand why spiritual warfare is so different from natural warfare. For instance, in the natural world, when you discard war, you have peace. However, in the spiritual world you have peace only when you declare war. So the only way you can have peace with God is to declare war on the devil; and when you declare war on the devil, he declares war on you.

So that is why it is imperative to have good boots on; because as you walk through this life, you will walk through thorns of temptation and thistles of tribulation; you will step in landmines of lust; you will have to scale mountains of misery. But if you have your feet shod with the preparation of the gospel of peace, you can remove every thorn and scale every mountain.

The word "preparation" literally means, "to be ready." Thus, when you are at peace with God, and you have the peace of God in your heart, you can deal with anything the devil throws your way.

Remember that it is not what happens to you in life that is important; it is how you respond to what happens to you that actually matters to God. If you are at peace with God, you can weather any storm that may come your way; for God's Word says in Isaiah 26:3, "God will keep him in perfect peace, whose mind is fixed on Him." Charles Wesley, the great hymn writer, once wrote:

> I rest beneath the Almighty's shade,
> My griefs expire, my troubles cease;
> Thou, Lord, on whom my soul is stayed,
> Wilt keep me still in perfect peace.

Now his feet were evidently shod with the preparation of the gospel of peace.

CHAPTER 7

THE SHIELD OF FAITH
REPELS THE DART OF DOUBT

We are instructed to take "the shield of faith with which you will be able to quench all the fiery darts of the wicked one" (Eph. 6:16, NKJV). The shield that Paul was referring to here was not the small, round shield that we usually picture in our mind. He was referring to the shield the Roman soldier would carry. This shield was very large—usually about two feet by four feet. It was made of wood that was covered with cloth and leather. Many times, this defensive weapon was dipped in water so that the fire-tipped arrows would be extinguished when they struck the soldier during battle.

I personally believe that this shield is to repel the dart of doubt. The Word of God says, "without faith it is impossible to please Him (God)" (Heb. 11:6, NKJV). Therefore, if faith is what pleases God, then doubt is what pleases the devil; and nothing thrills the devil more than to get Christians to doubt. First, he will try to get you to doubt God's word. Then, he will try to get you to doubt God's will. Lastly, he will try to get you to doubt God's work.

I want you to know unapologetically that there is nothing sinful and nothing wrong with doubt. Some people and even some preachers of the Gospel think it's a sin if you doubt. However, faith assumes doubt. In other words, if there is no room for doubt, then there is no room for faith. Do not ever be ashamed if you have had doubts in your heart. In fact, let me be totally candid with you. I have doubted. I have even doubted my salvation at times.

I even know some Christians who profess that they have never doubted their salvation; and honestly, I do not understand it. I once heard about a woman who approached Dwight L. Moody and said, "Mr. Moody, I've been saved for 25 years and I've never had a single doubt." Dwight L. Moody replied, "Madam, I doubt you've been saved. That would be like somebody saying, 'We've been married 50 years and never had an argument.' I doubt if they've ever been married."

Understand that doubt, in and of itself, is not a sin. It is what you do with your doubt that establishes whether or not it becomes a sin. Let me ask you a question: Do you know what doubt is? Someone has defined doubt as "a cloud that stands before the sun, keeping it from shining its light." Yet, doubt is a chance to fortify your faith, and the way you starve your doubt is to feed your faith. For that reason, you need God's Word to feed your faith. Romans 10:17 says, "Faith comes by hearing, and hearing by the word of God."

When doubt travels down your road, you just plainly need to say, "I am going to take God at His word and live according to His truths and principles no matter what." What is wrong with many of God's children today is they take up the shield of feelings instead of taking up the shield of faith. Now the shield of feelings is fine provided that you feel good; but when you start to feel badly, the shield of feelings will crumble right before your very eyes. The only shield that will repel the dart of doubt is the shield of faith.

The very next time Satan tries to bring doubt into your heart, look him in the eye and say, "Do what you will, but regardless of the situation, I am going to trust God and confide in His Word." When you do that, you will have just put up a shield he cannot infiltrate. Faith is the victory that triumphs over the world.

CHAPTER 8

THE HELMET OF SALVATION
REPELS THE DART OF DESPAIR

Just as the breastplate was to protect the heart, the helmet was to protect the head. The Apostle Paul tells us to "take the helmet of salvation" (Eph. 6:17, NKJV). In a war the two most vulnerable targets for any enemy are your heart and your head. If a soldier is injured in either of these places, he will likely die. That is why a helmet has always been one of the most vital pieces of the armor.

If the devil cannot invade your heart, he will try to invade your head. He will try to play mind games with you. He will either try to make you think you're lost, or he will try to convince you that you can lose your salvation. Then the first time you sin, he will say to you, "See what I told you. You have lost your salvation. You might have been a Christian, but you're not now; you've completely lost it." There is not a more depressed man in the world than a Christian who thinks he has lost his salvation.

When that happens to you, you need to put on the helmet of salvation. What is this helmet? It is, initially, the fact that you are saved, and secondly, the certainty that you can never lose that salvation. Did you know the Word of God teaches two things about salvation? It teaches, first of all, that you can be sure of it; and number two, that you can be secure in it. The next time Satan gets you to doubt whether or not you are saved, let me give you a good piece of advice: don't look back at a past occurrence. Don't look at how you used to believe. Don't pull out a church membership card or baptismal certificate. Pull out God's inerrant Word. Just turn to John 5:24, which says, "Most assuredly, I say to you, he who hears My word and believes in Him who sent Me has everlasting life, and shall not come into judgment, but has passed from death into life." In that one verse Jesus expresses two significant truths: You can be sure of your salvation, and you can be secure in that salvation. In other words, you can be certain you have eternal life, and you can be confident you will never come into judgment.

In his book, *Light for Anxious Souls*, George Cutting told about a farmer who lacked the assurance of salvation. He foolishly prayed that as evidence of his acceptance, the Lord would cause ten sheep of his flock—and only ten—to gather in a certain shed out in the pasture.

Later that day, when the farmer anxiously approached the shed, he was relieved to find exactly ten sheep. That gave him a temporary sense of peace. Doubt returned with the shocking thought that it may have been just a coincidence. So he asked the Lord that ten different sheep might gather in an opposite corner of the pasture. And they did!

When the farmer was asked, "Did this give you assurance?" he said, "No, nothing gave me certainty until I got the sure Word of God for it."

Cutting concluded, "He was all in a fog of uncertainty until he planted his foot firmly on the 'Thus saith the Lord.'"[5] That is truly taking up the helmet of salvation.

CHAPTER 9

THE SWORD OF THE SPIRIT
REPELS THE DART OF DISBELIEF

Our final weapon is "the sword of the Spirit, which is the word of God." Keep in mind that while armor is extremely crucial for the protection of the soldier, the warrior would be hopeless in battle if he had no weapon with which to attack the enemy and to defend himself. The first five weapons were defensive. The last one is offensive, for God does not always want us to be on the defense; He wants us to be on the offense as well. General George Patton once stated, "You fight a war attacking from the front, not defending from the rear."

We are specifically told to take the sword of the Spirit and go on the attack. The sword that Paul was referring to here was a short, straight sword that was used for close combat by the Roman soldier. It was about 14 inches long, sharp at the end and on both sides. It cut both ways, and this sword that we have is the Word of God. This makes us think about what the author of Hebrews wrote in Hebrews 4:12, "For the word of God is living and powerful, and sharper than any two-edged sword, piercing even to the division of soul and spirit, and of joints and marrow, and is a discerner of the thoughts and intents of the heart."

We all need to carefully understand that we have a defense for every weapon he has, but Satan has no defense for the one weapon we have. Therefore, when we put on the "whole" armor of God, we can shield ourselves against every attack of Satan. However, when we take up the sword of the Spirit, which is the word of God, he cannot shield himself against us.

Think about how Jesus defeated the devil when He was tempted in the wilderness. He only used one weapon—"It is written." He just took the sword of the Spirit and cut Satan through and through.

Our problem is, too many people keep their sword in the sheath and never pull it out. In a nationwide survey of Americans, the Barna Research Group found that 58% do not know who preached the Sermon on the Mount. Most Americans cannot identify the names of the first four books of the New Testament. Half of all adults (52%) did not know that the book of Jonah is in the Bible. Half of all adults (48%) did not know that the book of Thomas is not in the Bible. Seven out of ten adults did not know that the expression "God helps those that help themselves" is not contained within the Bible.[6]

So let me state the obvious. A sword must be removed from its sheath. It must be taken from its scabbard if it is going to be of any use. In fact, it has been said that a closed Bible is no better than no Bible at all.

Martin Luther preached a sermon in 1531; and although this message is over 400 years old, he said something in it that I want to convey to you as we think about this warfare:

"Christendom must have people who can beat down their adversaries and opponents and tear off the devil's equipment and armor, that he may be brought into disgrace. But for this work, powerful warriors are needed who are thoroughly familiar with the Scriptures, and can contradict all false interpretations and take the sword from false teachers-that is, those very verses which false teachers use, and turn them round upon them so that they fall back defeated. But as not all Christians can be so capable in defending the Word and articles of their creed, they must have teachers and preachers who study the Scriptures and have daily fellowship with it, so that they can fight for all the others. Yet each Christian should be so armed that he himself is sure of his belief and of the doctrine, and is so equipped with the sayings from the word of God, that he can stand up against the devil and defend himself when men seek to lead him astray."[7]

If you will take the armor of God daily, and from head to toe put it on, and then go do battle with the sword of the Spirit, I guarantee you that you will live a victorious life in Christ Jesus.

PART 3

MAN YOUR BATTLE STATIONS

Finally, my brethren, be strong in the Lord and in the power of His might. Put on the whole armor of God, that you may be able to stand against the wiles of the devil. For we do not wrestle against flesh and blood, but against principalities, against powers, against the rulers of the darkness of this age, against spiritual hosts of wickedness in the heavenly places. Therefore take up the whole armor of God, that you may be able to withstand in the evil day, and having done all, to stand.

Stand therefore, having girded your waist with truth, having put on the breastplate of righteousness, and having shod your feet with the preparation of the gospel of peace; above all, taking the shield of faith with which you will be able to quench all the fiery darts of the wicked one. And take the helmet of salvation, and the sword of the Spirit, which is the word of God; praying always with all prayer and supplication in the Spirit, being watchful to this end with all perseverance and supplication for all the saints... (Ephesians 6:10-18, NKJV).

If you are a part of the armed forces, especially the Navy, you will be familiar with the command "MAN YOUR BATTLE STATIONS!" Each time a service officer hears this, he knows to get to his post, lock and load, and make sure the safety is off, the trigger is pulled back, and he is ready to shoot and equipped to do battle.

I explained to you earlier that every born-again believer on this planet is at war. We are born at war with God because we are born in sin. However, when we lay aside our arms at the cross of Jesus Christ in total surrender, God declares peace with us. Moreover, when God declares peace with us, the devil declares war on us and we have to be continuously at our battle stations from earth to heaven. Understand that it is one thing to be willing to wage a war, but it is another thing to realize how to win it.

You can have the right weaponry, and you can be in the right position; but if you don't have the right strategy, you will always lose the battle. The Apostle Paul has expressed to us who our enemy is. He has told us what our weapons are, but now he shares with us exactly how to win the war. He teaches us how to unmistakably defeat the enemy.

CHAPTER 10

COMMENCE THROUGH GOD'S STRENGTH

Paul tells us to "be strong in the Lord and in the power of His might" (Eph. 6:10, NKJV). Now notice he didn't tell us just to be strong, but rather to "be strong in the Lord." This is not a matter of becoming physically fit. In other words, it is not physical exercise but spiritual discipline that matters if we are going to be equipped and eager soldiers of Jesus Christ. Thus, we are not to fight in our own strength, we are to fight in God's strength.

So often I have tried to win people to Christ, and perhaps the number one reason people give me as to why they refuse to accept Christ is something to this effect: "There's no need for me to invite Jesus Christ into my heart because I could never live up to His standards. I could never stay faithful to God; it is just too hard to live the Christian life."

Let me give you some fascinating news. The Word of God never teaches it is hard to live the Christian life. The Word of God teaches it is impossible. However, that is the whole purpose of being saved; because the moment you get saved, God gives you the strength to live the Christian life. If I could accomplish what God wanted me to on my own, I wouldn't need Him. If I could live the Christian life by my own strength, I wouldn't need God's strength. But the fact is, when you give your heart to Jesus Christ, He fills you with His Spirit; He gives you His strength; and it is only through that strength, and in that strength, and by that strength, and with that strength, that you are able to live the life that God has called you to live.

Now let me give you some bad news and some good news. The bad news is you cannot win this war in your own strength. You cannot beat Satan in your own strength. The good news is you don't have to because this war is not to be fought in your strength, in your own power. In fact, you cannot fight Satan in your strength, and that is part of the problem that many Christians are having these days. I honestly believe most Christians who even try to put up a fight against Satan, do so in the power of their flesh—do so in the might of their own strength. They try to outwit him. They try to outsmart him. They try to outmaneuver him. And the fact of the matter is, you cannot outwit a serpent, and you cannot outfight a lion. You can only meet Satan and defeat Satan in the strength and power of God. If you are living more in defeat than you are in victory, it is essentially because of two reasons. On the one hand, we neglect to recognize our shortcomings. The reason many of us don't pray is that in our heart we don't really believe we need to pray. We think because we're saved and we've got a good job, a stable income, a healthy family, and things are going well at work, we really don't need God. We regard God as someone you call on only in case of an emergency. Sometimes we have the attitude: "God, if I need you, I'll let you know!" However, isn't it interesting that when you get to the point in your Christian life where you think you are the strongest, you are actually the weakest?

Now please understand that there is plenty of room for self-assurance in the Christian life, but there is no room for self-dignity. The Lord Jesus said to Paul in 2 Corinthians 12:9, "My grace is sufficient for you, for My strength is made perfect in weakness." But then Paul added in verse 10, "For when I am weak, then I am strong." It was when Paul realized his weakness that he apprehended his strength.

As you examine the lives of the great men of God throughout history, you will find they were men who recognized their shortcomings. They recognized that without the Lord Jesus Christ, they could do absolutely nothing. Someone has well said, "Trying to live without God is a burden too heavy for man to bear."

On the contrary, we not only fail to realize our shortcomings; we then fail to depend on God's sufficiency. In and of ourselves, we do not have the strength, the power, or even the fortitude to fight this war and win it. But God does. There is a great question in God's Word that says, "Who is sufficient for these things?" Well, God is. We are reminded in 2 Corinthians 3:5, "Not that we are sufficient of ourselves to think of anything as being from ourselves, but our sufficiency is from God." The dilemma so often is that God is our last resort, rather than being our first resource. I have to be honest; sometimes in my own life, I will try everything before I'll try prayer. We will coordinate, demonstrate, regulate, activate, and scratch the bottom of the barrel of our human resources. When we try to do these things, we get what men can do; but when you try prayer, you get what God can do. A young boy traveling by airplane to visit his grandparents sat beside a man who happened to be a seminary professor. The boy was reading a Sunday school take-home paper when the professor thought he would have some fun with him. "Young man," said the professor, "if you can tell me something God can do, I'll give you a big, shiny apple." The boy thought for a moment and then replied, "Mister, if you can tell me something God can't do, I'll give you a whole barrel of apples!"[8]

Today, most Christians are losing the war because they have never sought God. Now without God you cannot win the war, and with God you cannot lose the war. But many of you are losing because you have never equipped yourself in His strength and in His might.

Notice once more in verse 10 that we are instructed to fight Satan "in the power of His might"—not the power of our might, not the power of our church's might, not the power of our pastor's might. We are to fight Satan in the power of His might. So that raises a question: How do you get this power? How do you get this might? How do you gain this strength in the Lord?

There is only one way you can have power with God: you must know God. Daniel 11:32 says, "The people who know their God shall be strong and carry out great exploits." It doesn't matter how hard you try, how righteous you live, how much you do, how vigilant you are; if you do not know the Lord, and I mean genuinely know the Lord, you are a 97-pound weakling in a 1,000-pound war.

There is only one way that you can get to know God, and it's the same way you get to know anybody: you have to spend time with them. You must have that quiet time. You have got to have a devotional life where every day you just get alone and have heartfelt fellowship with God. Because your quiet time, your devotional life, is not only where you get strength for the battle, it is where you succeed in battle.

Now I want to warn you of something. The devil will do everything he can to keep you from having that quiet time, because that is the secret to winning. That is the secret to happiness. That is the secret to peace. That is why you must indeed make that quiet time a priority—in fact, the priority in your Christian life. That is the ultimate source of being strengthened in His power and might.

Andrew Bonar, a great man of faith, had three rules for his successful life: Not to speak to any *man* before speaking to *Jesus*; Not to do anything with his *hands* until he had been on his *knees*; Not to read the *papers* until he had read his *Bible*.[9]

That is why Andrew Bonar was such an incredible soldier of the cross and was triumphant in his war.

CHAPTER 11

COMMUNE IN GOD'S SPIRIT

In Ephesians 6:18, Paul states that we are to be "...praying always with all prayer and supplication in the Spirit, being watchful to this end with all perseverance and supplication for all the saints...." Now be aware that what comes last is certainly not least. The reason that Paul is going to end this passage on spiritual warfare by calling God's people to prayer is because prayer is the battle. Therefore, you are not getting geared up to do battle when you commune with God in prayer. Prayer is the battle. It is on the battlefield of prayer that the war will either be won or lost.

If you will allow your mind to go back to the garden of Gethsemane, you will remember that it was there that Jesus faced one of the greatest battles of his life. In fact, it was there that he told his disciples that they had to stop and pray. And although Jesus won the battle for sin on the cross, He won His battle for the cross on His knees in prayer in the garden of Gethsemane.

The real aim concerning the war that we are fighting is this: The battlefield is prayer. The war is not fought on your feet; it's fought on your knees. That is why if you are a Christian who never prays, seldom prays, or halfheartedly prays, you have "given up" in your war without even firing the first shot. It will be a wonderful day when we understand that the devil is not afraid of our sermons, our singing, our services, or our stewardship; but he is afraid of our prayers. If the devil can do only one thing in the church, he will keep the church from praying. He does not fear buildings, budgets, or baptisms. It is prayer that Satan disputes; it is prayer that Satan despises; and it is prayer that Satan dodges. The armor of God is worthless unless it is invigorated by the power of prayer. In truth, it is better to have a strong soldier in weak armor, than a weak soldier in strong armor.

Do you know what the awful tragedy is about prayer? It is not unanswered prayer; it is unasked prayer. Now think about this for a moment. When we pray, the devil cannot keep God from answering, so he tries to keep us from asking.

Perhaps many of you still may not realize why prayer is a battle. However, if you will think for just a minute, you will understand why prayer is the battle. Who is Satan's war with? His war is not with you or me; it's with God.

In Revelation 12 we are told about a war that once occurred in heaven. It was a war that was waged between Satan and God. Furthermore, it was God who cast Satan and one-third of the heavenly hosts into the pits of hell. It was God that eternally damned Satan and his army. Therefore, Satan's war is not essentially with us; it is with God. However, Satan knows that he cannot harm God. But if you want to harm someone, and you know you cannot reach them, the very next thing you try to do is to harm someone that the person loves. That is the reason Satan engages in war with us and attempts to do us harm, because he is trying to harm God in the process. That is the wonderful thing about communing with God in prayer; because when we continue in a spirit of prayer, we take the battle that Satan is taking to us, and we hurl it back where it belongs, into the hands of an omnipotent God.

When it looked as though Israel was going to be conquered by the Assyrian army, King Hezekiah stood before the people and declared, "With him is an arm of flesh; but with us is the Lord our God, to help us and to fight our battles" (2 Chron. 32:8, NKJV). God is not interested in your battling for Him; He wants to do battle through you. When you commune with Him in prayer, you unleash the power of God in the fight.

CHAPTER 12

COMPLY WITH GOD'S STRATEGY

Three times in Ephesians 6 we are charged to stand: in verse 11 we are told to "stand against the wiles of the devil", in verse 13 "having done all to stand", and in verse 14 Paul begins by saying, "Stand therefore". Now that's a very odd request, because here you are equipped from head to toe with the armor. You are now out on the battlefield of prayer, you are marching back and forth, and you can scarcely wait to go on the attack. You are ready to strike and you are just waiting on the command. Finally, your orders are delivered. You excitedly open up the envelope and find that you are commanded to simply "STAND FIRM!" We are not ordered to attack, we are just ordered to stand firm. Now why is that? Well, when you take a stand for God, you won't have to go to war; the devil will bring the war to you.

Do you recall in Daniel 3 the glorious story of those three brave young men named Shadrach, Meshach, and Abed-Nego who wholeheartedly loved the Lord Jesus? Do you remember how a law was passed that everyone in the country would have to bow down and worship the golden image of King Nebuchadnezzar? Now these three men did not initiate a violent demonstration. They didn't carry out an intense protest. Yet, when everyone else bowed down, all they simply did was stand up. Just because they took a stand for God, war was waged against them.

One of the primary reasons America is in the shape she's in today is because God's people have been bowing down before the gods of this world, instead of taking a firm stand for the cause of Jesus Christ. For way too long God's people have been sitting calmly on the sidelines, instead of standing courageously for the Savior.

Please realize that God is not looking for Christians who can do spiritual cartwheels, jump pews, swing from chandeliers, speak in tongues, perform miracles, or do any number of other things. God is merely looking for people who will stand firm and stand up for the Lord Jesus Christ. In fact, God is not looking for Christians who can run fast; He is looking for Christians who can stand fast. He is looking for those who can stand true and remain faithful even when the battle is over and the smoke has cleared.

I know that some of you might have the mentality, "Well, if I stand for the Lord, I'll make enemies." And that is certainly true. Nevertheless, the friends you make by taking a daring stand will have more admiration for you than the friends you make by straddling the fence. Now there is only one of two things a soldier can do when the fight becomes intense. They can advance or retreat.

The only reason a soldier ever retreats is out of fear. However, "God has not given us the spirit of fear, but of power and of love and of a sound mind" (2 Tim. 1:7, NKJV). If you will go back and look over this armor, you will find there is not one piece of armor for the back of a Christian. Now why is that? Because God's soldiers are never to run from the devil; they are to resist the devil.

After the tragic bombing of a marine base in Beirut in October 1983, the steadfastness of one young soldier moved and heartened the American people back home. He had been critically wounded in the explosion of the revamped hotel where he and his fellow marines had been staying. Many of his buddies had been killed. He was covered with bandages and a jungle of tubes was attached to his body. He could not speak. Yet when he was visited by General Paul Kelly, Commandant of the Marine Corps, he indicated he wanted to write something. Painfully he wrote the words "Semper Fi," a shortened form of the U. S. Marine Corps motto, Semper Fidelis. It means, "Always faithful."

May we man our battle stations, stand firm against the devil, and fight him in the power of God's might, while always remaining faithful so that we can defeat the enemy and have inevitable victory in Christ Jesus.

ENDNOTES

PART 1

[1] Churchill the Warrior, *The Churchill Centre*, July 26, 2005, http://www.winstonchurchill.org/i4a/pages/index.cfm?pageid=692.

CHAPTER 3

[2] James Merritt, "Are You Going To Be There?", *Touching Lives*, July 31, 2005, http://www.touchinglives.org/articles/areyougoingtobethere.htm.

[3] Geoffrey C. Ward, *The Civil War*, (New York: Alfred A. Knopf, 1990), pp. 150-168.

PART 2

[4] The New England Journal of Medicine 1999; 340: 1930.

CHAPTER 8

[5] *Our Daily Bread*, April 28.

CHAPTER 9

[6] J. Kirk Johnston, *Why Christians Sin*, (Grand Rapids: Discovery House, 1992), p. 68.

[7] Charles Swindoll, *Sanctity of Life*, (Dallas: Word, 1990), pp. 101-102.

CHAPTER 10

[8] *Today in the Word,* April 1989, p. 43.

[9] Keith L. Brooks, *Essential Themes,* (Chicago: Moody Press, 1974), p. 6.